Candid

A Memoir

Sheryl Nicole Prince

DEDICATION

To the hurting hearts in hiding, healing is
in vulnerably living your truth and walking in your
authentic purpose.

CONTENTS

ACKNOWLEDGMENTS

Benayih, thanks for your continuous love, support, and encouragement babe. Your feedback and input have been invaluable. I love and appreciate you beyond words and beyond measure.

Phara, thanks for being your DOPE self. I don't know what I would have done without the expertise and support you've selflessly provided. You're truly a blessing lady, love & hugs!

Rachel, thanks for always sharing your insight and wisdom with me. It challenges me to elevate my thinking and explore endless possibilities. I love and appreciate you Napoleona!

Lisa, thanks for helping me give birth to my "baby" *Candid*. Those last few moments of labor were agonizing, but your calm, prayerful nature helped me pull through. Love, hugs, and blessings in abundance lady.

Thanks to my loving family for supporting me in sharing my story, our story. We've come a long way individually and collectively. Our bonds and love for one another grows deeper and stronger with each passing day. I'm blessed and grateful to God for giving me such a beautiful family. I love you all beyond words, beyond measure, and forever.

SHERYL NICOLE PRINCE

CHAPTER 1: FIRMLY PLANTED

God drew me near
Whispered in my ear
My child do not fear
I will always be here
Share your testimony for all to hear

Perfectionism is a debilitating disease
In fact, it's a strategic attack of the enemy

A calculated plan to delude,
confuse, and impede
You from living your purpose
and walking into your destiny

MASK OF PERFECTIONISM

For years, I hid behind my education, degrees, and my success. I presented as an intelligent, ambitious, and accomplished woman who had it all together. Yes, I was all of that and then some, but I damn sure didn't have it all together. I wasn't even close to having it all together. I was simply hiding behind these things to cover up my past, which I had "hidden" so well.

I was ashamed of my past. Ashamed of how I grew up and the things I went through. Ashamed to speak my truth because I was worried about how people would perceive me. I didn't want anyone to have pity on me or laud my accomplishments because of what I had overcome. The veil of shame became a mask of perfectionism. A mask that threatened to suffocate the life out of my body.

No matter how "perfect" I appeared, my past still loomed and lurked about. It reminded me of people, things, and situations that I tried desperately to erase from my memory. It haunted and deeply traumatized me. It simply refused to be quietly tucked away. Its voice cried out to me, wailing for freedom. A cry that pierced my soul and could no longer be ignored. It was time to take off the mask.

Laying shame aside
No longer can I hide
Behind the lies
Time to uncover what's deep inside

JOURNEY

A journey across seas
To the beginning of me

Back to humble beginnings
But this journey signifies the ending

Time rewind
Leaving it all behind
No longer will I be confined
Freeing my mind

Things of old
Will release their hold
No longer will I be controlled

New creation
Different destination
Headed for greatness

SHHH

Hey Lil Cuz!
Oh, I see
You're washing the area from where you
pee
Lemme help you soap it up real good
Shhh be quiet, understood?
Just helping you wash it, okay
Shhh, don't ever tell anyone about this day

What the hell, why did you tell
Now they're all mad
I even got a beating from my dad
I thought we were fam
Damn!
Betrayed my trust
Just a little lust
Oh wait, I was wrong?
I don't have reason to sob this song?
'Cause now although I'm gone
The hurt and pain I caused lives on
Sorry Lil Cuz, please forgive me
I should've never touched the area
from where you pee

SHERYL NICOLE PRINCE

"VICTIM"

Daddy's gone
Mama's torn
Tries to escape through the drugs she's on
Taken from home
To a place unknown
Brother and sister separated
Subjected to molestation
In the church house preaching & teaching
Late nights feening & creeping
Sunday morning calling people to the altar
Monday night kissing the lips
of your foster daughter

Because you kissed me
Your wife dissed me
Called me a liar and dismissed me
Rock the cradle you lying little bitch
Punished for being a "snitch"
Cradle rocking til the early mornin'
Cause it's me her husband yearning
Hush little baby I'm beyond tired
Shut the fuck up and keep rocking
you little liar
You know what, I'm sick of this shit
I didn't cause it
It's your husband's fault, him and his dick

Morning finally came
School bell rang
Days passed
But I couldn't get past
The ordeal
So I squealed
Removed from the home
That was worse than my own
Foster care system
Misplacing children; Victims
Of circumstance
But I decided I had a fighting chance
So I gave it my all
And can stand tall
To tell this story to all of y'all

TAKEN FROM HOME

I remember the car ride to my foster home. The strange lady, my brother, and I rode in silence for most of the trip. From time to time, we'd break the silence with questions we demanded answers to. *Where are we going? Why are you taking us away? Where is our mother?* In the awkward moments of silence, I stared out the window wondering about my whereabouts. Wondering about my mother. Wondering what was going to happen to my brother and me.

It all started when Mommy took us to the foster care agency one day to seek help for her drug addiction and to get money for food. She'd previously gone alone with my aunt, and they'd provided her with financial assistance. But this time around, it was a completely different situation. They placed my brother and me in a playroom while they spoke with Mommy privately. Something didn't feel right to me. I wasn't interested in their damn toys; I wanted my mother. I wanted to go home!

But we didn't go home that night. They took us to live temporarily with our maternal aunt. They allowed Mommy to follow us in a cab to my aunt's house and say her goodbyes, promising that she'd see us soon. My intuitive eight-year-old mind fully comprehended what was going on. They deemed Mommy as an unfit parent and took us right from under her nose. We thought we had eluded the system when they came to the school asking about our home environment and Mommy's habits, and I lied and told them that Mommy only smoked cigarettes and drank beer sometimes. But this time they caught us and captured us.

Over the next 7 years, I was shuffled between 4 foster homes. I lived separately from my brother in the first 2 foster homes. My first foster parents are the subject of my poem **"Victim"**. "Good ole church folks" on Sunday;

predator and victimizer on Monday. Even at my tender age, I refused to be their victim. I knew what they were doing was wrong, so I opened my mouth and reported the incident just like I reported when my cousin touched me inappropriately.

I was removed from that home and placed with a lovely couple who welcomed me with open arms and hearts. They were good people who provided a loving home for me. However, my foster father and his sister-in-law abused drugs in the home. They thought they were discreet, but I had seen and heard a lot growing up in my home environment. So, I knew when they were "secretly" abusing drugs behind the closed door, emerging with eyes that betrayed them every time. My foster mother didn't indulge, but she didn't seem to intervene either. My little mind couldn't comprehend how I was taken from my home where drugs were abused and placed in a foster home where guess what, drugs were abused.

My brother and I were finally reunited in my third foster home. It was the best feeling in the world to be reunited with him, living under the same roof together again. Ironically, we didn't spend much time under that roof though. Our foster parents often locked us outside in the backyard with their two rottweiler guard dogs. We would escape and run the streets of Brownsville, boosting along the way. Just like at home, we had very little supervision and were left to our own devices.

We were placed in another foster home that was much more structured, too structured perhaps because sometimes it felt like a boot camp. Food and toilet tissue were rationed out. Sunday showers were timed and closely monitored; on other days, we washed out of a bucket in the sink. We could only use the upstairs bathroom when we needed to move our bowels, and we couldn't flush the urine in the downstairs bathroom. We were confined to the basement, where she closely supervised us until it was our bedtime. She was a feisty, older lady whose intentions were good and whose heart was in the right place, although some of her methods were a bit questionable. I guess she was doing her best to foster seven children under one roof while trying to keep the bills to a minimum.

No child wants to be removed from their home and separated from their family. It is a frightening, traumatizing, and life-changing ordeal. Furthermore, some foster parents and their home environments are not conducive to nurturing children. But then, there are those who effectively foster the development of children in their care and love on them in the absence of their parents. Those are the moms and dads that deserve praise, accolades, and blessings in abundance.

SHERYL NICOLE PRINCE

BIG SHERYL

My mother was a baby herself when she had me. Puppy love between two teens gave life to Sheryl Nicole Prince. Neither my mother nor my father were ready or equipped for the responsibility of being parents. They were still growing and learning themselves. But on June 24, 1980, I made my grand entrance into the world. Ready or not, I was here!

Before drugs entered my mother's life, she was a good mom doing the best she could to raise two children at the tender age of eighteen. Our home environment was loving, nurturing, and structured. She groomed us well and dressed us in the cutest outfits. She kept our bellies stuffed with her good cooking. Every night she bathed us with such care before tucking us in for bed. She was also our first teacher. I knew the alphabet, how to write my name, and could read little books before I even entered kindergarten. My mother was doing a hell of a good job raising my brother and me by herself as a teenage mom.

I noticed a change around the age of 6 or so. She would be holed up in her room by herself or with her friends. When she would emerge, a funny smell permeated the air. Her appearance and behavior were off. She was also laxer with my brother and me; our daily routine changed over time.

When the drugs took over, life changed drastically for us all. Locked behind her bedroom door, my mother abused drugs more frequently. Sometimes she'd lock us in the house, leaving us to our own devices. We'd light her cigarettes and take a few puffs before putting them out. One time, we even drank some vodka that we found in the refrigerator. Refusing to be pent-up, we found ways to escape so we could run wild and free.

Our home environment was spiraling out of control to say the least. My mother no longer cleaned, cooked, and nurtured my brother and me as she once did. We often had to fend for ourselves, so I stepped up to care for my younger brother. We were thick as thieves and had each other's back, side, and front. We were inseparable, basically conjoined as we navigated our new "norm" together.

The only time we were separated temporarily was when I went to school, leaving him at home with my mother. I took school seriously and went every day, although my mother didn't make us go. I would rummage through dirty clothes, get dressed, and go to school. School was my safe haven and my escape. I excelled and was in the top classes. I loved coming home and teaching my brother what I had learned. You couldn't tell me I wasn't a teacher lol. Who knew then that one day I would in fact become a teacher?

I remember being at school one day when I

was taken into a little room for questioning. There, I was interrogated by presumably a child welfare social worker. She asked question after question about my home life. *Is there food to eat at home?* Yes. *Does your mommy beat you?* No. *Does your mommy do drugs?* No, she only smokes cigarettes and drinks beer sometimes. When she realized she wasn't getting anywhere, the interrogation stopped, and I was allowed to go back to class. I ran home to tell my mother about the incident. I don't remember her reaction or response, but I remember being afraid that they would come to take my brother and me away from her.

One day, my fear was confirmed. They removed us from our home and temporarily placed us in the care of our maternal aunt. She lived in the same apartment complex as us, so we weren't too far from our mother. My mother would come to visit us, and we would see her in passing on the street. But it wasn't the same as living under the same roof with her. I didn't live under the same roof with her again until I was 21.

Unfortunately, we were removed from my aunt's custody and placed into foster care. Over the years, my mother visited us at the agency. She came pretty regularly, 80-90% of the time. Sometimes she brought other relatives with her. I especially loved when she brought my little sister with her. She was born 2 years after we were removed from home and had been adopted by my aunt. On special occasions like birthdays, my mother held a big party for us at the agency. My brother and I always looked forward to her visits and longed for the day we would be able to go home with her.

It was the worst feeling when it was time to go, and we had to part from her. I would break down each time, and she'd console me and reassure me that she'd see me soon during our next visit. The times she didn't come for our visits, I was inconsolable. My brother would chastise me for crying; then he'd try his best to console me. My social worker, on the other hand, often added fuel to the fire. She'd make snide, unprofessional remarks about how my mother was choosing drugs over my brother and me. I would argue her down viciously and defend my mother. How dare this bitch talk about my mother like that? I hated her guts and was often rude, defiant, and non-compliant as a result.

She didn't know what the hell she was talking about. My mother not only came to visit us at the agency, but she also attended all of our graduations. She even went to the IEP meeting when my brother was being evaluated for special education services. Furthermore, she was enrolled in a drug treatment program, and she was also taking parenting classes. She was doing what she needed to get us back, but seemingly it was never good enough for the folks at the agency. I personally believe that my mother and social worker's hostile relationship impeded the process of us returning home. Consequently, we didn't return home until we were adults.

At the age of 21, I returned home to live with my mother. Unbeknownst to me, she was still struggling with substance abuse. She would run the streets all day and come in late night reeking of drugs and alcohol. Some days/nights I'd go looking for her to bring her home. One time in particular, I hunted her down to get the money back that she'd "borrowed" from me. On another occasion, I remember finding her drug paraphernalia and trying to destroy it. As the plastic medicine bottle slowly melted, it burned my fingertips, but I was too focused on destroying her chances of getting high to notice.

Of course, destroying her drug

paraphernalia didn't put an end to her substance abuse. But one day, she took a bad batch of drugs that had her bedridden for two to three days. She later told me that she felt like she was dying and promised God if he spared her life, she'd give her life to him. That was the turning point and the beginning of her new lease on life. She sought drug rehabilitation and began disassociating with the people she formerly ran with. She began attending church and rededicated her life to Christ. She also went back to school to train to become a chef.

I was so proud of her and rooted for her every step of the way. Of course, I was front and center, cheering the loudest at her graduation ceremony from the culinary arts program. And when she began working, I'd take her to and from work as my schedule permitted. On the weekends, we spent some much-needed quality time together doing the things we loved. We devoured her tasty meals, watched movies, went shopping, visited loved ones, and attended church. God had healed, delivered, and restored my Mommy.

September of this year will make 18 years that my mother has been substance-free. I marvel at her strength and resilience to master sobriety. I spoil her every chance I get with lots of love, flowers, gifts, vacations, etc. She deserves it and then some because she's been to hell and back but has remained strong, resilient, and grounded by her faith. Having survived drug addiction, she also beat breast cancer's ass not once, but twice in the last 4 years. Big Sheryl is one tough cookie, a fighter who perseveres in the face of adversities. I'm so proud to be Lil Sheryl and have inherited many of those same qualities.

So when she tells me that I inspired her to get her life on track because she saw how hard I worked going to school and work each day, I tell her that it was her who inspired me because I've witnessed her fighting spirit all my life, and as her namesake, I could only embody and emulate the example she set.

#QUEEN

Sometimes your crown becomes
shifted or twisted

Sustains chips, cracks, dings, and dents
May even become bent

Yet it remains intact and affixed
A testament of your strength

Daughter of a King
You reign supreme
You are #QUEEN

Holding everything together
when you feel like you're falling apart
Queen, you're truly a work of art

A masterpiece indeed
Giving tirelessly
Loving selflessly

Doing it all with a smile on your face
While struggling to hold your
crown in place

Daughter of a King
You reign supreme
You are #QUEEN

What was meant to break you, shaped you
What was meant to fold you, molded you
What was meant to bend you, mended you

Still here, still standing
Presence ever so commanding

Can't help but shine
You're divinely sublime

Daughter of a King
You reign supreme
You are #QUEEN

Live out loud
Live boldly
Live purposefully
Live wholly

Always look heavenward from
whence your help comes
The Mighty One and The Son

Eyes & feet forward
Pointed towards your destiny
The best is yet to come so give
God the Glory

Daughter of a King
You reign supreme
You are #QUEEN

ANGEL

I vividly remember making the life-changing phone call. I was standing in the kitchen of my foster mother's house. *Grandma, do you know anyone who can take us in?* I asked. *They're gonna place us in a group home if we can't find anyone.* My voice trembled as I choked back tears. *I have an aunt in Queens, I'll ask her,* she replied. *Okay, let me know because we can't stay here anymore.*

Our time had run out at our foster home. The house we called "home" for the last 5 years no longer welcomed us. The woman we called "Mommy" could no longer mother us. She was getting older, so fostering teenagers who were growing defiant was becoming too challenging for her. Consequently, my brother and I were facing the possibility of being placed in a group home. We had heard horror stories about group homes, so we definitely didn't want to be placed there. We were scared

33

and felt hopeless.

Our social worker suggested that we call everyone we knew to see if they could take us in. My paternal grandmother was one of the first people that came to mind. She was caring for my cousins in her home, so unfortunately, she couldn't take us in. But maybe she knew someone who could. Lucky for us, she knew the perfect person.

Aunt Gwen was my grandmother's aunt. They grew up together in St. Croix, USVI. They were only 2 years apart, so they hung out together and were more like sisters than niece and aunt. So, my grandmother knew she could count on Aunt Gwen to care for my brother and me. Without hesitation, Aunt Gwen agreed to take us in. She and her husband would provide a home for us, rescuing us from the perils of the group home system.

My brother and I were 13 and 15 respectively when we went to live with Aunt

Gwen. Nana, as she affectionately became known to us, was the matriarch of the family. She was strong, wise, nurturing, and loving. She raised us like we were her own children. In fact, we were; she adopted us and made it official. We had finally found our forever home.

Life with Nana was full of many new, wonderful experiences. I had a spacious, beautiful room all to myself. I was enrolled in ballet, hip hop, African, tap, and Jazz dance classes at the neighborhood dance studio. Nana sent me to get my hair done at the salon biweekly. I also had the best Sweet 16 surprise birthday celebration ever. I felt at home and loved for the first time since being removed from my mother's home.

Nana's wisdom and the many teachings she shared from her own life experiences were invaluable. We'd sit in the kitchen as she prepared dinner and candidly talked about any and everything (school, boys, sex, etc.). During our kitchen talks, Nana imparted so many words of wisdom and valuable teachings that I still hold dear in present day; morals and values that have shaped me into the woman that I am. Lessons about love (especially self-love), not settling for less than you deserve, working hard to get whatever you want out of life, and so much more.

I'm forever grateful to my Nana for opening her home and her heart to my brother and me. I'm equally grateful for the instrumental part she played in preparing me to be the woman that I am today. Our relationship and bond will forever be strong. Our love will continue to grow exponentially. She will forever be my angel.

Beauty is your name
God's beautiful masterpiece
Beauty inside out

His eyes behold you
His most perfect creation
Embrace your greatness

GREATNESS

Being me ain't easy
This shit is hard
But it was written amongst the stars
You see, HE chose ME

I was destined for greatness
From birth
When I made my grand debut on Earth

He planted the seeds
Believe, achieve, succeed
Learn, grow, prosper
Fight, overcome, conquer

So I've been running my race
At my own pace
Many hurdles along the way
But God has the final say

"Glory to my name"
"You're destined for greatness"
He has proclaimed

"My daughter, greatness resides within"
"Sheryl Nicole, you will win!"

PERFECTLY IMPERFECT

Tryna be perfect and do
everything perfectly
Is impossible and exhausting so I quit
I'm done with this dumb shit
I'm perfectly imperfect
In all of my ways
Done wasting my days
Tryna be "Lil Miss Perfect"
'Cause this shit ain't worth it
Comes with more than you bargain for
Time to show that bitch to da door
'Cause perfect is impossible
Improbable
Unattainable
Unrealistic
Sadistic, when you think of it
Paining yourself to be perfect
Just ain't fucking worth it
When you'll never be anything but
perfectly imperfect

BROWN GIRL

Go 'head Brown Girl sing your blues
For all the world to hear

Let em stare
Let em jeer

Maybe they'll even cheer
One thing for certain they will hear

Truth untold, will unfold
Kaboom, EXPLODE

Bottled it all up til it overflowed
Spewing out with no control

Speak up Brown Girl
Let your voice be heard
Utter the words
Racing through your mind

Busting at the seams of your heart
Fighting to escape the tight grip on your
throat

Bottled in, let it loose
Speak your truth

No guilt, no shame
Bring glory to His name

Anxiety, depression, uncontrollable
thoughts fought
Blessed to the son, YOU won
So speak up Hun

CHAPTER 2: PURPOSEFULLY PRUNED

I don't write to be deep
I simply write to speak
My mind in eloquent rhymes
Spit a few lines
A verse or two
Purposed to
Inspire you

MOST HIGH

40 years
Countless tears
Anxiety, depression & fears
Wondering why I'm still here
Then it became clear
I have a testimony others need to hear

Some tell their story for fame
Others tell it for financial gain
I simply want to bring glory to His name
And witness that because of Him
I overcame

What was meant to destroy me
Kill me, take me out
Victoriously I will open my mouth
and shout

About the goodness of God
That brought me this far
Never would have made it
Without God on my side
So I give praises to the Most High

Aimed for my head
Thought I'd be dead
But instead
I survived
I thrived
I AM ALIVE!

I BELIEVE IN BLACK LOVE

Black men have disappointed and hurt me, beginning with my own father. Some have used, abused, and mistreated me. Others didn't know how to love or appreciate me. Yet, I love Black men with a passion. That will never change.

I'm not bitter or jaded by my past. I don't subscribe to the notion that Black men ain't shit. I chose the ones I dealt with. My hands aren't clean. I am undisputedly the common denominator in all of my relationships and dealings with Black men.

Those experiences, whether good or bad, have made me better. They've taught me to love deeper and harder, and to love myself unconditionally. I simply want to be the best Queen for a deserving King. I wholeheartedly and unequivocally believe in Black Love.

BABY GIRL

I remember dreading visits Upstate to see my Daddy locked up like a caged animal. I'd sob uncontrollably and hide in the comfort of my elbow as I laid my head on the table in the visiting room. My mother would try her best to get me to engage with my father, but I was often uncooperative. I was a shy, sensitive kid and didn't know how to interact with him. I also didn't like going to the facility; jail was a depressing and scary place. I was vocal about my feelings and pleaded with my mother to let me stay back when she went on her visits with Daddy. She eventually stopped dragging me along.

When I was about 13, my dad was released from prison. He would visit us at the foster care agency and bring us all sorts of gifts and goodies. He promised to get us out of "this place" and provide a home for us. Our hearts were filled with hope. Hope that was quickly dashed away when my dad was incarcerated again. He had made a promise that he couldn't keep.

I felt like a balloon someone had stuck a pin in. I was quickly deflated as easily as I was pumped up with false hopes and promises. The excitement, the joy, and the anticipation were all gone. Doom, gloom, and sadness filled me. Then hurt, anger, and resentment crept in. How could he do this to us? Why didn't he try harder to stay out of trouble so he could provide a home for us as he promised?

I carried those feelings and questions around for years to come. When he was released during my mid-twenties, I took the opportunity to ask the questions I had wondered about and to express the pent-up feelings I carried for years. There was remorse on his part, so I had to practice forgiveness. It wasn't easy because I still felt the sting of the hurt and pain caused by his actions. But I tried my best to put it aside and forge ahead with us getting to know one another and building a relationship.

Over the years, we've worked on learning one another. We've had our ups and downs throughout the process; I choose to highlight the good moments instead of the rough patches. The moments when my Daddy made me feel like his little girl. Flowers and candy for Valentine's Day. Early morning texts wishing his "baby girl" a blessed day. Playful rivalry as we watch Sunday football games, rooting for our opposing teams. Moments that we continue to create as we foster our evolving relationship.

HEARD

How will my voice sound
reciting these poems
Only my heart and mind
have ever known 'em
They live freely there
Living life without a care
No need for an intrusive ear
Can't they just stay there

Unless I dare
Utter a word
Then they'll be heard
Foiling the plan of the enemy to steal
And savagely kill
My destiny and purpose
So I refuse to allow them to
remain unspoken
Throat tight, I feel like I'm choking
Stricken with fear
Gasping for air
I speak the words
That need to be heard

ENCORE

The smile on my face wasn't genuine. You'd think I had so much to be happy for and to smile about. I was celebrating my 30th BDAY, had been reunited with my father after decades of separation, and had just graduated with my second Master's degree.

I was happy about my accomplishments, but I was unhappy about where I was at in life. Separated from my then husband, I was forced to move in temporarily with my parents while I looked for a place of my own. I had never lived with my dad before, so it was a huge adjustment to say the least. Learning and living with a "stranger" was challenging.

I tossed and turned most nights on the air mattress on my parents' living room floor. Overcome by life's curveballs, I cried myself to sleep many nights. Weeping may endure for a night, but joy comes in the morning was the furthest thing from my reality.

Every day I put on a brave face and suited up with the armor of God simply to go teach my "babies". I was the target and obsession of an administrator who abused her "power" and sought vengeance for no perceivable wrongdoing on my part. Sheer incompetence masked by bullying and intimidation tactics. Fighting back intensified the attack, but I fought back with everything in me daily despite the many other battles I secretly fought.

Exhausted from combat, I would rush home to retreat and gather myself before the chaos of family life began. Uncontrollable tears often overflowed during my stolen moments of "peace" in the comfort of my parents' empty, still apartment. Other days gospel music filled the air, and I belted out praise and worship as if my life depended on it. Then I'd hear the key in the door, no time for an encore..."

TOXICITY

I once did a drug
It was called LOVE
Had me high, had me strung
Had me beside myself
It was detrimental to my health
Mentally, emotionally, spiritually
Quite emphatically
Until I broke free
From the toxicity
And wisely chose me

BLESSING

I once met a conman who charmed his
way into my heart.
I should've known better from the start.

Freshly broken heart,
still licking my wound.
Not thinking, I moved on too soon.

Swoon, I fell into his cocoon!
Entangled in his web, on me he fed.

I would soon dread the mistake I made
when I failed to use my head.
Too late, I was sleeping with the enemy
in my bed.

You shouldn't get married so quick.
What if he just wants citizenship?

But he can't find work without any papers.
Smoke and mirrors, vapors.
You're living together and going to church.
Stop living in sin and just make this work.

On bended knee, he proposed to me.
I said "Yes" foolishly.

Almost half-heartedly
Because I knew intuitively.

This wasn't the best decision
So I hid it.

We did it
With just one witness.

Justice of Peace, Court house
Kept as quiet as a mouse.

'Cause of shame
I didn't take his last name.

Mine remained
Things changed.

Hardworking, ambitious, driven
Going to school while busting my
ass to make a living.

Breadwinner, he fixed dinner.
Then resentment entered.

Accusations of superiority
A coverup for insecurity.
Arguments, fights
Eventually he didn't come to bed at night

Phone calls, texts, and pics
Looking for a new home for his dick.

I was sick, straight done with the shit
So I called it fucking quits!
Pack your bags and go
You're not welcome here no mo'!

For better or for worse
I chose me first

Letting go hurt
Healing took time and work

I don't regret the experience
It increased my resilience

Taught me my worth
Gave birth

To the woman I am today
"Perfect" in all my ways.

Scars, flaws, and imperfections
Simply known to my #KING as
his blessing.

I'M GOOD

MY friends would say
you're damaged goods
Repeat that again
I think I misunderstood

Who the hell are they
And why do I give a fuck what they say
Tell me, which bills of mine do they pay

And why the hell they give a damn
about with who you lay
Pardon me if I'm in the way

Of this bromance
Nah fuck it, you never had a chance

You could never tap this ass
And this shit wouldn't last

Cuz I lost interest just that fast

Why? YOUR friends are stuck on my past

Yes I was a wife
But decided I didn't want that life of strife
Nor did I want a man
That didn't have a plan
And couldn't stand
On his own two feet

So I chose me

I'm good
You're understood
Wish you well
Oh, and tell your friends to go to hell

RESTART

Why do fools fall in love
Because love is like a drug
High, floating on clouds, distorted reality
Eyes wide open but you can't see
Blinded to L-O-V-E
Heart and mind out of sync
Mind doesn't clearly think
'Cuz your heart rules
Seizes control over you

Master of your fate
Impatient, refuses to wait
Overpowers, devours
You
Abused
Misused
Confused
No longer belongs to you
You freely gave
what you should have guarded
Because no one regarded
Your most precious treasure
Squandered away for selfish pleasure

Carelessly abused and bruised
Refused to be accused, so you excused
The misuse
Foolishly blamed it on you

Until your mind, unblinded by the lies
Caught up and subdued
Your reckless heart
Defibrillated it back to life
Restart

NEW LOVE

I loved him but I loved me more
So I showed him the door
'Cause love didn't live there anymore
Whole again, down to my core
New love, I'm ready to explore
With someone who will adore
ME
And love me sincerely

BELOVED

I am blessed with a beautiful, Black man
who loves me for me
When he looks at me, my true
beauty he sees
He loves me wholeheartedly,
unconditionally

My flaws are my perfections
My scars are marked blessings
Battle wounds, he gently soothes
Carefully dressing them with love
Undoubtedly, I am loved
Just as I am, all of me
Absolutely unequivocally

LOVE MAKING

As you kiss me I fall deeper
into your embrace
I feel the warmth of your breathing
on my face

All over my body your hands
roam and caress
Finally landing on the fullness of my
breasts

Feelings akin to sensual pleasure
As I feel the rising of your manly treasure

Clothes off, skin to skin
Then I feel the penetration
of your manliness deep within

Together we race to reach that peak
We hold each other, proclaim our love
In each other's arms, we peacefully
fall asleep

FUSION OF THE HEARTS

How sweet it is to be loved by you
A love that is so pure and true
Evident in all that you do

You guard my heart with
impenetrable protection
Your deep love for me is truly a blessing

You help me heal past hurt and pain
Promising to always remain

By my side, through it all
Pledging your love will never falter
That it cannot be altered

Because this love is forever
Sent from above by the
Mighty One in Heaven

God divinely arranged our timing
Paths crossed, meeting of the hearts
A beautiful start
His masterpiece, a magnificent work of art
Inseparable fusion of the hearts

A LOVE LIKE THIS

I never knew a love like this before
Unfiltered, raw
Unadulterated, pure
That good kinda love
Make you smile deep down to your soul
Permeates your body from your head to
your toes
A love so good, everybody knows
Your radiant glow shows
What your heart holds
Joyfulness
For a love that you never knew to exist
One you're unable to resist
Sealed it with a kiss
Holy matrimony
Vowing to be each other's one and only
Til death do us part
You'll always have my heart
Until from this world, I finally depart

MATTERS OF THE HEART

Battles fought
Scars deep
Hurt and pain began to seep
To the inner most part
Matters of the heart
Threatened to destroy this work of art

YOU'RE FIRED

I'm not one of those people who thinks seeing a therapist means you're crazy. On the contrary, you're "crazy" if you think you don't need therapy, especially after having a traumatic experience. If you don't deal with trauma, it will indeed deal with you. It will manifest itself in so many areas of your life, and in so many ways. Your relationships and career may be severely impacted. Hurt and pain will turn to anger and bitterness, which may lead to sickness and disease. Therapy helps you address and deal with trauma so that it's not a toxin to your peace, or a dead weight holding you down.

I have gone to therapy as far back as I can remember. The foster care agency sent us to see a therapist on a weekly basis. I received group and individual counseling for about 4 years straight while at my last foster home. My therapist was a middle-aged Caribbean man who was relatively an effective therapist, in addition to being a father figure to me.

But I wasn't healing because I tried to conceal the trauma so that I wouldn't have to relive the hurt and pain. As I stated before, what you don't deal with will deal with you. My relationships, both personal and professional, were affected. Anger and bitterness caused me to lash out at others. Broken trust and past disappointments caused me to be very distrusting of others. Pent-up emotions eventually led to anxiety, panic attacks, and bouts with depression.

Triggers, such as loss of control and impending doom, led to an increase in anxiety and panic attacks. I especially noticed the increase during stressful times such as divorce, homelessness, issues on the job, etc.

I finally decided that I needed to seek help because my anxiety and panic attacks were snowballing out of control. Cognitive therapy helped me to uncover and explore the things that I had buried, the things that were at the root of my anxiety and panic attacks. I quickly learned that what's "buried" will always resurface again.

Finding a therapist I could relate to, and whom I could trust proved to be more difficult than I imagined. During grad school, I was counseled by a student clinician in training who was really good. She helped me to explore the things I buried deep inside. She was also instrumental in my life at a time when I needed someone to talk to about my feelings around being separated from my now ex-husband. I looked forward to our sessions because they challenged me to do the work necessary for my healing. Unfortunately, I lost touch with her once I graduated from the university. My search for a quality therapist resumed.

Over the years, I've met some mental health

"professionals" that were anything but professional. There was the Russian psychologist who could not seem to get past the fact that I defied the odds of my torrid past to achieve success. She harped on it every chance she got, which made me feel uncomfortable, mainly because it almost appeared as if she expected me to be a statistic instead of a success. So, I fired her. Next!

Then there was the young, white clinical social worker who lacked professional decorum and diagnosed me as having "Major Depressive Disorder" after I shared with her during my intake that I recently had the worst bout with depression I ever experienced. When I challenged the diagnosis, she flippantly chalked it up to not being a "big deal" and stated that she would just change it. I called her out on her careless attitude, which she tried to justify by stating she didn't subscribe to the labels the DSM-IV applied to people, so she didn't get caught up on diagnoses. Dissatisfied with her response, I followed up with her white, male supervisor who unsuccessfully attempted pacifying me by complimenting my achievements. Needless to say, their services were no longer needed.

Lastly, there was the Caribbean female psychiatrist who was more interested in gossiping about her colleagues. During our intake appointment, she spent more time inquiring about my interaction with the young, white clinical social worker than discussing my psychological needs. My counseling needs were placed on the back burner because she was more concerned with where I shopped for clothes and the things I had accomplished in my "young years". She seemed to marvel at my accomplishments while looking for holes in my story. Once she was done prodding, she diagnosed me with PTSD and sent me on my way.

Despite these negative experiences, I still

value mental health services. I understand and have experienced first-hand the importance of these services. So, I am optimistic that one day I will find a therapist that is the perfect fit for me. A therapist who can relate to me and understands my counseling needs. A trained professional who will help me flourish during the healing process.

ATTEMPTED ASSASINATION

If I was the Devil I'd aim for your head too.
Assassinate and destroy the most
important part of you.
Head filled with dreams, creativity,
promise, and purpose.
Annihilate it all, make you feel worthless.
Hopelessness, despair
Anxiety, depression, fear
The end is near
Then you hear:

"The enemy's attack on your mind
Should remind
You of my promises
Don't let him convince
You they don't exist
You must resist
Satan and he'll flee from you
Persist and do what I equipped you to do".

VICTORY

Daughter, let me fight this battle
It's not yours
I am the Mighty Lord
So it belongs to me
It's me against the enemy
Feelings of inadequacy
Insignificance
Are all tricks of his
To make you feel unloved
Although love pours in
abundance from above
Anger
Unforgiveness
Tricks to keep you in bondage
But through me
You are set free
As long as you believe
Anxiety, fear, depression
Tricks to keep you from your blessings
My child, take up your weapons
My Word, prayer, praise
Shall keep you all of your days
In them you'll find me
And have sweet, sweet victory

SAVIOR

I refuse to let anyone or anything
take me back to the place I prayed
my way out of.

Escaping because of His love and
help from above.

Darkness enveloped me.
Anxiety, fear, and depression choked me.
But the Word provoked and woke me.

To His deep, immense love for me
Evident in His never-ending
grace and mercy

Not forsaken or condemned
Although I was riddled with sin

He stretched his arms wide
Allowing me to retreat and hide
While healing the vast hole inside

Wiped the many tears I cried
Brought to life the passion
I thought had died

Gave me back my hope, strength, and fire
Promised me my testimony would inspire

YOU
To walk in your purpose and
live out your truth

CHAPTER 3: LEVELS OF ASCENSION

MUTHAFUCKING # QUEEN

Knocked down, counted out
The enemy cried a victorious shout

But Queen, adjust your crown
Keep your head up, never look down

Head high, middle fingers higher
FUCK the devil, that filthy liar

Said you wouldn't make it, that's a lie
Lemme break it down
Check it, here's why

What was meant to break you, shaped you
What was meant to fold you, molded you
What was meant to bend you, mended you

Still here, still standing
So hold your head high, chin up
Shoulders back
Tell 'em who the fuck

You are, you're a star
Can't help but shine
You're divinely sublime

Live out loud
Live boldly
Live purposefully
Live wholly

Always look heavenward from whence
your help comes
The Mighty One and The Son

Eyes & feet forward
Pointed towards your destiny
The best is yet to come so give
God the Glory

Daughter of a King
You reign supreme
You are a muthafucking #QUEEN

I LOVE ME SOME HER

She's been through some things
Experienced lots of pain

Felt buried, never to see the sun
But by His grace and mercy she's overcome

Trials, tribulations, adversities
Depression, anxiety,
overthinking tendencies

Planted not buried
Blooming, blossoming
Growth, transformation

Mentally, emotionally, spiritually
I love me some her unconditionally

POPPIN'

Memories, Facebook memories. I was reminded today of a memory from 2016. The first thought that came to mind was, "2016 was the year my curls were POPPIN". But my eyes told a different story. They were sad and tired. 2016 was one of the best/worst years of my life. I don't know how that's possible, but that was my reality.

I was a Level 4 Senior Education Administrator earning six-figures. I was finally putting my 2nd Master's to use and making the money all of my hard work deserved. But I wasn't happy. I thought I could impact change on a large-scale in my position, but bureaucracy and nepotism stood in the way. Folks in high places wanted me to subscribe to and maintain the status quo and cheat our "babies" out of the quality education they deserved.

I was in a district where sadly, many folks basically came to kick up their feet. A district where students who weren't successful in a traditional high school setting needed teachers, administrators, and staff to give their all and be their best because this was the last stop on the bus for these "babies". A district where court-involved youth were seemingly "inducted" into the prison system instead of rehabilitated. Yet, the district was littered with mediocre, subpar, and half-ass "educators". Head honchos "protected" their teacher friends from little ole me who was shedding light on and speaking out against the bullshit.

I was a threat to the status quo. I refused to sit behind my desk, twiddle my thumbs, and just collect my six-figures quietly. I was at Rikers Island and juvenile detention centers every week advocating for black and brown boys. I pushed and challenged teachers to improve their instructional practices in order to maximize instructional outcomes for students. I was a voice for voiceless students who didn't know how to speak up or advocate for themselves.

I became a target for simply doing my job. Doing it well might I add. Too well in fact, because I was disrupting the status quo. As a result, I was warned, reprimanded, and even received counseling memos about my "performance". *That's not your job*, I was told. *There are people whose job it is to…*. they continued. So, you mean to tell me that if folks aren't doing the job they're getting paid to do and I do it in service of students I'm in the wrong?

Tired of fighting a seemingly losing battle, I jumped off the sinking ship. I took a position as an Assistant Principal (AP) in a K-5 school. My time as an Assistant Principal was short-lived. After months of interviewing for the position and going through the entire C-30 process before being officially hired, I resigned after 3 short months. Yup, I quit my six-figure salary job because I had reached a breaking point.

The Principal was smarter than smart and knew her shit. But at times, she lacked basic people skills. Her motives were questionable too. She knew the work environment I had just left and promised that things would be different under her leadership. That was the bold-face lie she told.

As a new relationship does, it started off really well. But the honeymoon phase didn't last long at all. Although I arrived at work each day before 7am and stayed past 6pm most days (9pm on some occasions), she didn't appreciate my hard work and dedication. She was demanding, condescending, and vindictive. I didn't like or condone how she spoke to the staff, especially the other Assistant Principal. He seemed to be used to it and just went with the flow. I, on the other hand, refused to go with the flow.

In the short time that I worked there, incident after incident led me to reach the conclusion that it was not going to work long-term. On one occasion, she sent me to the basement to "help" facilitate the collection of student record files. Shortly after sending me to the basement, she called for me to come up to the main office to make an announcement over the Public Address (PA) system. When I reached the office, she was there sitting directly in front of the PA system. Annoyed, I made the announcement as requested and retreated back to the basement. A short while later, I received an email notification on my phone; there was a message from her stating that my tone was unpleasant and unprofessional during my announcement. Later that day, I spoke with her regarding the email, and she casually brushed it off as "feedback".

On another occasion, she and I conducted a classroom observation to observe a teacher's instructional practices. From the moment we entered the classroom, she began finding fault with everything and openly criticized the teacher. At one point, she even admonished the teacher in front of her students about the placement of the projector and roughly demonstrated to her how she wanted it placed. Later, she told me to write-up the observation and provided me with some "infractions" she wanted me to include in the write-up. When I insisted that she write it up instead because our perspectives differed, she retorted that I would not walk around "playing good cop versus bad cop". Furthermore, she remarked that I would "get some blood on my hands", so I should be prepared. I was horrified by her statement and made no qualms about expressing how the situation affected me.

That was definitely a turning point in our

professional relationship. Things escalated to me resigning from my position at the start of the following school year. Over the summer, as I read her menacing and harassing emails with project deadlines that infringed on my personal time during summer vacation, I decided that I had had enough. I could not and would not continue to work under her "leadership". I was tired of her and supervisors like her abusing their "power". I was also tired of the bureaucracy within the education system. So, I resigned and decided to pursue my aspirations of entrepreneurship. It was the most liberating and the absolute best decision I ever made.

MIRRORS OF MY SOUL

My lips may lie
But my eyes can't hide
The hurt and pain I feel deep inside

Mirrors of my soul
A reflection of what my heart holds
Trauma never told

Things my lips may never speak
Secrets my eyes cannot keep
They'll always tell the tale
That my heart knows so well
Even when I try to conceal it
My eyes can't help but reveal it

SUPERWOMAN

Fuck the lies that were told
This superwoman shit is played out and
old

Jeez, for her fucking sake
Give superwoman a muthafucking break!
Or into little pieces she'll break

Bend and fold
From weight she wasn't meant to
carry or hold
What an unbearable load
Many hats, different roles

Expectations, demands, pressure
More pain than pleasure
Unguarded treasure

Buried so deep
HELP, SOMEBODY SAVE ME!
I CAN'T DO THIS BY MYSELF
CAN'T YOU SEE I NEED HELP

ARE YOU TOO BLIND TO SEE
I TAKE CARE OF EVERYTHING BUT ME

She cries out in vain
But no one understands her pain
"You got this girl!"

"Go save the world."
"Wipe them tears and put that cape
back on."
"You're the one we're all counting on."

Tears rolling
Weight of the world she continues holding

Superwoman needs saving
But has no help
She's expected to save herself

LEAP OF FAITH

Leaving my 8-4 and pursuing entrepreneurship was one of the best decisions I have ever made. As a dedicated employee, I worked long, grueling hours. I worked diligently and tirelessly towards whatever goal my employer set, even if I didn't necessarily agree with it. I always went above and beyond to get the job done. In the process, I sacrificed so much of myself for so little in return. I eventually came to the realization that my hard work and tireless efforts were not appreciated. I was tired of not being valued, tired of the bureaucracy, and tired of people abusing their "power".

I always had dreams of becoming an entrepreneur and running a successful business one day. But I played it safe like school and society teaches you. I went to school, earned 3 degrees (2 Master's), and finally landed a position with a six-figure salary. But I wasn't happy and felt unfulfilled. I knew I could do so much more for students and families, but not within the confines of a suffocating system. I felt as though I was expected to sit on my hands and be a puppet on a string. I had not gone to school for all those years and worked so hard to be anyone's puppet. I wanted to produce large-scale change how I best saw fit, so I took a leap of faith.

Many people thought I was crazy for leaving my six-figure salary position to embark on entrepreneurship. However, although I made good money, I wasn't happy. Furthermore, I could make six-figures or more working for MYSELF, with MY same education, experience, and skill set. I knew that it wouldn't happen overnight, but I was determined to bring it to fruition one day. If I could work tirelessly and diligently to bring other people's goals to fruition, I could do the same for myself.

I got my first taste of entrepreneurship working as an Independent Contractor for an educational services agency. The Jewish lady who ran the agency was cool, but she operated in the best interest of her business, not mine. I provided Special Education Teacher Support Services (SETSS) at 3 different schools throughout upper and lower Manhattan. I worked Monday-Friday from 8-4, had 25 students on my roster, and only made about $25,000 that school year (minus all the money I spent for gas and parking). As a new entrepreneur, I made less than a quarter of what I made as an Assistant Principal, but I wasn't deterred.

I wisened up the second year that I worked with the agency. I only worked cases in Brooklyn, 15-30 minutes from home. Also, I had about half the number of students I previously had on my roster. I informed the agency owner that I wanted to keep my schedule "light" because I was working on my other business ventures (I had launched a travel agency through an MLM company, followed by the launch of Sheryl Nicole). But one day, she called to tell me about an enhanced rate case that was "good money", which she was offering $49/hr for. I reiterated that my business ventures were my top priority, but she was intent on me taking the case, so she offered $50/hr. I agreed, but she later reneged on her word, telling me some BS about it wasn't feasible for her to pay me $50/hr. I continued working the case for my student's sake, but I decided to leave the agency because she foolishly decided I wasn't worth a measly dollar.

I was determined now more than ever to be my own boss. I applied with DOE to become an independent SETSS provider. I thought the application process would be tedious, but I was approved in a matter of a day or so. As fate would have it, I retained the last client I took on from the agency I previously worked for. I was both excited and nervous about this new chapter in my life. Excited because I had finally taken the next step, nervous because my earning potential looked bleak initially.

The excitement began to wear off as I struggled to build my clientele. I was pulling in only about $800/month with the one case I had. Cases weren't just dropping in my lap as I guess I thought they magically would. So, I took a job with a specialized school for students with special needs. I lasted about 3 days because I was immediately overwhelmed by the systemic issues and bureaucracy that were beyond my control. I refused to go back to square one, so I quit and began exploring other options.

I decided to take on enhanced rate cases with an agency that was willing to pay me

$60/hr. I was over the moon happy until I learned that the City was paying them almost $130/hr, while they paid me less than half of that. Was I not the one in the field working with these students with severe special needs? Wasn't I also the one that was subjected to deplorable conditions in some of my clients' homes? Yet, they were perfectly fine paying me less than half of what they received as compensation. It was time for a change!

By this point, I realized that simply having my name listed in the directory of providers was not enough. I needed to be more proactive about building my caseload and my clientele. I began contacting the various Committee on Special Education (CSE) offices to let them know I was a provider with availability in my schedule to accommodate their students. One CSE in particular immediately connected me with a school that was in need of a provider. There were 12 students on the caseload, and the school was less than half an hour from the other school that my first client attended. The classroom I would soon call home was very inviting, spacious, and full of resources and materials. Most of the staff welcomed me, the Principal was easy to work with, I was made to feel at home, and I loved my babies and their families. God had opened up the windows of heaven and poured me out a tremendous blessing.

Things were beginning to look up for me. Although my personal life was in chaos (I was dealing with anxiety, depression, and homelessness), my professional life began to flourish again. I had previously "shuttered" Sheryl Nicole temporarily because it was difficult running a business while bouncing from couch to couch and combating mental health issues. I also ended my relationship with the MLM company because I no longer wanted to deal with a middleman who took a percentage of what MY hard work and efforts earned. I became focused on starting my own comprehensive educational services agency; it was my turn to employ others.

In July of 2019, I finally incorporate *Elevated Youth*, my educational services agency. I housed my *Enterprising Youth Entrepreneurs* (EYE) program under my newly formed corporation. EYE was piloted that June, to educate and expose youth to entrepreneurship. My goal is to hire well-compensated contractors for *Elevated Youth*, who will deliver exceptional educational services tailored to meet each family's unique needs. I also plan to get EYE in school districts throughout the city and beyond.

Serial entrepreneurship has become my passion; it's in my bloodline. I recently launched a cleaning business, *Prince Cleaning Services*, in memory of my late paternal grandparents; my grandmother was a domestic worker and my grandfather was a serial entrepreneur. My goal is to create generational wealth and leave a legacy for generations to come. I also want to empower, equip, and inspire others to do the same. If I can do it, anyone can do it.

Entrepreneurship and my life, in general, have been a roller coaster ride. It has taught me so much about myself and the world in general. I've grown tremendously as a person by operating outside of my comfort zone and being "comfortably uncomfortable" while tackling challenges and taking on risks. Entrepreneurship has also helped me tap into my creativity, monetize it, and expand my reach; my love for writing is a prime example. Who knows, maybe I'll establish and operate a publishing company that caters to self-published authors such as myself one day.

Hey, I CAN do anything I put my mind to because by the grace of God, I DID accomplish the things I set out to. So, you CAN because I DID, and it should inspire you.

SLEEPLESS NIGHTS

Do you know sleepless nights
Because your dreams,
goals & aspirations savagely fight
For your undivided attention
And refuse to remain within

Dreams
Busting at the seams
Can't be contained it seems

At best you get a little rest,
but never for long
Cause your aspirations hurry sleep along
Goals lurk hungrily in your head
Starving you of sleep until they're fed

Achieved, completed,
conquered, devoured
They overpower
And control your life
Keeping you up, sleepless nights

NIGHT SKY

There's something about writing
in the stillness of the night
Surrounded by peace and quiet
One with your thoughts
Overwrought
When your emotions flow unrestricted
They need no permission
To cascade freely
Completely
No distractions, no competition
Nothing vying for your attention
Truth revealed, lies unconcealed
Mind, heart, soul allowed to heal
As your pen dances across the paper
Your labor
Of love unfolds
Your story is told
Bold
Colorful
Powerful
Like the night sky
Under which it peacefully lies

SIMPLY SHEY

I remember the days when fear paralyzed me; I was stuck on the ground level, not moving. I was so afraid of the huge undertaking of starting a lifestyle brand. Where would I begin? What should I say? Would I be relatable? Would I be accepted? Would people take me seriously? Do I have what it takes to garner the following of an audience? Would I even have an audience? How would they view me once I revealed all of me--flaws & fabulousness?

So, I focused on what was "easy", what came naturally to me. I put all of my time, energy, and efforts into building someone else's brand, all the while neglecting my own. I worked my ass off to make them richer, while robbing my own brand of a chance to even take flight. Sad to say, but that was the norm for me. I was good at selflessly and tirelessly helping others bring their vision to fruition, but I neglected to exert the same energy and effort to help myself. Or perhaps I choose to help others to take the attention off of myself. The "background" was a safe hiding place for the shame my past hung over my head.

Reality is a bitch; she makes you face her and own your truth. Truth is I was scared to uncover who Sheryl Nicole truly was, scared to step into my greatness, and scared to let my light shine brightly. But then one day I declared, "No more running, no more hiding, no more dimming my light--it's my time to SHINE!" Whether folks were ready or not, Sheryl Nicole was here! Like it, love it or leave it alone, I can only be me, simply Shey.

LOVE ME SOME ME

When you love on you,
you can't help but be your best self
Cuz ain't nobody gonna love
you like you love yourself
You see,
I love me some me
I had to fight to be the woman I am today
So I love her in all of her ways
Imperfections, flaws
I love it all
Quite simply,
I unapologetically love me some me

ROYALTY

I'm ROYALTY!
Can't you see?
Behold, feast your eyes on me

It's the captivating twinkle in my eye
You can't deny
The beautiful fullness of my lips
The sashay of my hips

My kinks, coils, and curls
More precious than diamonds,
rubies and pearls
Head beautifully crowned
Glistening skin, hues of brown

Wisdom, intellect, knowledge
My vast superpowers

Courage, perseverance, strength
The depths of me, to my fullest extent

It is my intent
To fully embrace my royalty
Because all of me
Deserves to be called "Your Majesty"

SIMPLY ME

My makeup is dope
I'm hella beautiful
Not Fenty, MAC, or Maybelline
Underneath, in between
Deep down inside, just simply ME

WHO I AM, WHOSE I AM

Comparison is truly the thief of joy. I will admit that I used to get in a funky mood when I saw others' success flash across my screen. Why them and not me? What do they have that I don't have? When will my time come?

Usually, as quickly as the mood came, it went because I reminded myself that my journey and my walk were MINE. I thought about all that I had accomplished by the grace of God and was reminded that I ought to be grateful for the countless opportunities, opened doors, divine connections, and abundance of blessings. I was then convicted to thank God for His many provisions. I began to count MY blessings instead of counting theirs. I didn't know the hell they had been through in pursuit of God's promises for their life. I didn't know the prayers they prayed and the time they spent with God manifesting the blessings in their life.

Nor did I know the time, effort or energy they put in to ensure their prosperity.

I could either be a spectator watching from the sidelines while they slayed the hell out of their goals, or I could roll up my sleeves and put in the work needed to slay my goals. I chose the latter. I refused to be a mere spectator when I am perfectly purposed to execute and excel. God placed the vision in my heart and equipped me with everything I needed to bring it to fruition. The only competition was the inner me who sometimes needs to be reminded who I am and whose I am.

A MILE IN YOUR SHOES

Jealousy is a debilitating disease
Feeble individuals displeased
With their own reality
Rather celebrate your downfall
instead of your victory
There's more that meets the eye
than they see
You fight ferociously with
the enemy and your "inner me"
They couldn't walk a mile in your shoes
Shit, some days you don't even want to
But you choose
To keep pushing 'cause you can't lose
You have too many people
depending on you
Strength renewed
You forge ahead
Don't let the haters get in your head
You're loved beyond measure
As valued as a bountiful treasure
So take pleasure
Because they too, recognize
your vast measure

NO RECIPROCITY

I root for others, even when they
don't root for me
Even when they act like their eyes can't see
And there's no reciprocity
But that doesn't stop me from being me
You see
I root for the underdog
The champion
Alike
I encourage them through their plight
'Cause I know the fight
Knocked down counted out
But the naysayers can't count
So give it all you got, every single ounce
Let's go, I'm rooting for you
Even though you ain't rooting for me too

ROOTING FOR EVERYBODY BLACK

I've come to the realization that not everybody wants to see you win. Sadly, it's often those closest to you, so-called family and friends. The main ones you'd expect to have your back and support you 100%. Especially when you've supported them without hesitation more times than you can count. Heck, you've bent over backwards and went out of your way to nurture their dreams. Now that it's your turn, the love and support are nonexistent.

I know it hurts like hell and upsets and frustrates you to no end. However, what can you expect from crabs in a barrel? How dare you "escape" and "leave them behind"? Who are you to get ahead while they remain stagnant and "stuck"? It's almost as if your winning prevents them from winning. But why can't we build, grow & win...TOGETHER? Why can't we break the vicious cycle and end the curse of generational poverty...TOGETHER? Why can't we build wealth and leave a legacy for generations to come...TOGETHER?

I'll tell you why, because some people are so narrow-minded and can't think outside of their self-imposed box. They don't comprehend how us helping one another benefits us all. They can't wrap their minds around the idea that it's not about competition, but about community. OUR community, the Black community. The community with the largest number of consumers but the least wealth. The community in which our dollar reportedly circulates for about 6 hours amongst Black-owned businesses before being pumped into more affluent communities who fully understand the science of cooperative economics and building generational wealth. We're too busy buying our wants and begging our needs, and trying to keep up with the Joneses' instead of building like the Dangotes.

That's why outsiders can come into our neighborhoods and swindle their way into buying property for dirt cheap, "develop" it, then rent/sell it to gentrifiers while essentially kicking us out. Yet, we still just don't get it.

Allow me to digress a bit because it baffles and frustrates me to no end. The systematic structures put in place to keep us in our "place" are successful because many of us refuse to open our eyes. We walk around oblivious, foolishly rocking designer blinders. Then there are the "woke" folks who might as well be asleep due to inactivity. Like really wake the f*ck up people! Stop perpetuating society's expectations of a mediocre existence for OUR people. Let's break these damn glass ceilings and tear the roof off this mutha!

It starts at home. Parents cultivate your child's dreams. Instill in them that the sky is truly the limit. Brothas and Sistas, support one another and sharpen each other as iron sharpens iron. Learn financial literacy, the importance of investing in land/property ownership, and stocks/bonds. Live a financially fit life and work diligently towards financial freedom. Support Black-owned businesses and buy Black. Let's connect, network, build & grow together Kings & Queens. Know that I support you and am rooting for you. I'm rooting for everybody Black and that's a fact!

MELANIN RICH

Loving me in spite of what society tells me
Skin too dark
Lips too full
Hair like wool

So called "inferior" to those "superior"
Lighter hue
Supposedly better than you

MELANIN RICH,
synonymous with disease
But I refuse to appease
Instead I celebrate the beauty that is ME

Coily curls, luscious lips
Darker hue
Simply beautiful

BLOODSHED

I'm tired
Of our black boys & men dying
At the hands of each other
By the hands of another

Lives lost in the blink of an eye
Why?
Is precious blood splattered
'Cuz someone decided his black life
doesn't matter

Decided he lacked value
That couldn't be further from the truth
He was a beautiful black man
Doing all that he can
In a society that taunted him
A cruel world that hunted him
His harsh reality haunted him
Consumed by strife
Fighting for his life
Snuffed out without thought or remorse
Sadly this was his plight

CAN I LIVE?

My mother and I were racially profiled in the middle of the movement, which was catapulted by the senseless murder of George Floyd by a white police officer. The experience left me physically, mentally, and emotionally drained. It prompted more questions than I had answers. Why can't I simply LIVE my life freely as others are able to do so? Why does my mere existence bother some people? Why am I viewed as a threat when it's MY very existence that's threatened? How could they pull a stunt like this at a time like this? So many questions swarmed my head causing it to throb with pain.

We had just finished grocery shopping at the supermarket located outside of Staten Island Mall. As we emerged, we noticed that the line to enter the store was growing as people made their early morning grocery store run in the midst of a pandemic. A police car sat at the end of the parking lot near the mall's entrance, for crowd control perhaps. My mother helped me unload my groceries into my car, then walked over to her car which was a few feet across the parking lot. I pulled alongside her as she loaded the handful of groceries into her car. I exited my car to hand her somethings I had for her from my backseat; a value pack of toilet tissue I had purchased for her 2 weeks ago and a skirt I wanted her tailor to fix for my upcoming birthday. She in turn handed me some items she had for me.

I felt the cops watchful eyes on us but ignored them. Then, they slowly began approaching us. By this point, we'd finished our exchange and were getting back in our respective cars to head to our next destination. I followed behind my mother; the cops followed slowly behind me. I didn't think anything of it until they suddenly switched lanes and drove past me, riding slowly behind my mother, but to her right. They appeared to be making a right turn, but when they realized we were going straight they continued following us. My mother and I were on the phone the entire time and concluded that they were probably running our license plates.

We entered the shopping plaza across from the mall with them in pursuit. They finally turned off and we continued on to our destination. The line was beyond ridiculous outside of the store we wanted to go to, so we decided we would come back another day. We exited the plaza and continued down the main road to our next destination. Unbeknownst to us, the cops followed us from a safe distance while we were busy strategizing our shopping plans. My mother was going to the pharmacy and I was heading to the dollar store, then we'd meet at the dollar store. When we met up, she told me that the same white cops had followed her to the pharmacy. They flashed their lights as if they were going to stop her. However, as she pulled into the pharmacy parking lot they suddenly backed off.

This boiled my blood! Why were they fucking with us for no good reason? Especially in a climate where police brutality was rising, and more and more black men and women were being savagely executed by cops. A time where protesters around the world were marching in support of the Black Lives Matter movement. A time where tensions were high, and riots broke out because folks were tired of injustice after injustice. So why were they racially profiling, harassing, and trying to intimidate two black women who were just running errands on a Saturday morning?

My head and my heart hurt. My blood boiled over. Just as it had done the time officers singled my brother's car out during a funeral procession when our loved one passed away. The cops were headed in the opposite direction of us when they saw a young, Black man with locs driving a nice car. This prompted them to bust a U-turn, cutting me off as I followed behind my brother in the procession. They instructed him to stop and pull over. When I emerged from my car to ask what the problem was, I was told to get back in the car, they simply wanted to check his license and registration. But I'm my brother's keeper so I persisted. I wanted to know why they were stopping him out of all the cars in the procession. My question was answered by a stern command to get back in the car. If it wasn't for my brother, I wouldn't have complied and retreated back to my car.

He told me to get back in the car and reassured me that "he got it". He gave the officers his license and registration as demanded. Sadly, as a Black man in America my brother was used to being stopped, harassed, and racially profiled by police. He knew to remain calm and compliant during the situation in order to walk away from it alive. Sadly, even when you're calm and compliant that doesn't ensure that you'll walk away breathing.

As a Black person living in America, you simply can't breathe. Especially when your killer has his knee on your neck restricting your breathing as you plead with him for your life. Or he places you in a deadly chokehold with no mercy for the soul leaving your body. It's sad. It's scary. It's heartbreaking. It's our reality as Black men and women simply living on this Earth. But it shouldn't be and doesn't have to be if we ALL take a stand against racism. Individually and collectively we must do our part to extinguish racism because Black Lives Matter and are valuable.

INTACT

No justice, no peace
Fuck the police
KKKrooked KKKops
Patrolling our blocks
Quick to pull their Glocks
And gun down a Black man
Because he can
Get away with cold blood murder
Cause apparently Black lives don't matter
Another life robbed of promise
and purpose
Because a gun was cowardly pulled

Bullets pierced the body of yet another
Black man, black woman,
my sister, my brother
They can take our lives in the blink
of an eye
But can never take our beings
Can't erase our existence, persistence
To rise above racism and hate
Death of the Black race will not be our fate
At their hands
They don't stand the chance
To control our future, our destiny
So it kills them inside

They bulk up their chest with false pride
Insecurity, inferiority they hide

Feed us lies
And try to deny
Our beams of light
Which they cannot hide
So bullets penetrate our
flesh poking countless holes
Yet they never destroy the
depths of our souls

FAITH

Over the years, my faith has kept me afloat. During the dark moments, my faith allowed me to trust that the sun would shine again. I reminded myself that there's ALWAYS light at the end of the tunnel. So, I kept praying, I kept pushing, and I continued to trust that God had my back. It didn't break me, so I knew I was going to experience a breakthrough. AMEN!

The devil comes to steal, kill, and destroy. He attacked my mind, body/health, joy, peace, family, relationships, finances, etc. Sometimes it was unbearable because I felt like I was fighting a losing battle. I could either take it lying down or fight back.

I chose the latter! I prayed, praised, and pushed my way through. It wasn't always easy, but it was necessary. Satan was relentless in his attack against me, so I had to be strategic and intentional in my counterattack. By the grace of God, I didn't succumb to warfare unleashed on me by the enemy. My faith in God's power to do exceedingly, abundantly above all I could ask or think helped me to endure and be victorious.

DISCONNECTED

I wish I could sail away
Like a balloon drifting into the heavens
I dream of meeting my Creator
In awe I stand of His greatness
I used to dream this dream
But not anymore
I seem to have lost my connection
No, it's me who has become disconnected

AMEN

I said a prayer today
At first, I didn't know what to say
My lips moved but I couldn't find
the right words
Because I haven't been filled
with your Word
Dry, barren, empty vessel
Succumbing to the flesh against
which I wrestle

Convicted, condemned
He won't blot out my transgressions
and sin
Resorted to not inviting you in
Disobedience blocked my blessings
Will I ever learn or will it continuously
 be the same repeated lesson

Tired of disappointing you,
breaking your heart
Father, please grant me a fresh start
In your Word and truth
I shall take root

Help me deny my flesh, put it aside
Stop feeding into Satan's lies
You said if I repent
You'll forgive me of my sins
So Father, I repent

Please help me rebuild your home within
My heart, my mind, my soul
Please Lord make me whole

I desire you
I want to do what you want me to
Less of me and more of you
Father God I believe victory I will claim
In your son Jesus Mighty
and matchless name
AMEN

HIS LOVING ARMS

For so long I suffered in silence,
thoughts running rampant
through my head
Cried myself to sleep, tear-stained bed
Hopelessness, despair, dread
Some days I'd think, "I'm better off dead"
But I'd never take my own life
Crazy how death seems more
bearable than the strife
The constant fights
With the enemy
With inner me
Filled with anxiety
Unable to sleep
Pen and paper help to ease
The debilitating disease
That robs you of your peace
Threatening to defeat
You, knocks you off your feet
To the perfect position
One of submission
To God's mighty power
You call on him in your hour
Of trouble and need
He's a true friend indeed
Wraps you in His loving arms
Keeps you safe from harm

Sends His angels to guard
Your mind and heart
Reminds you to not lean to
your own understanding
Acknowledge him and he'll give
you peace that surpasses all understanding
Peace flows like a river, calm
You finally fall asleep in His loving arms

SWEET VICTORY

He tried to tell me my voice
wouldn't be heard
"People don't understand the words
Coming out of your mouth, he lied
Your speech is tongue-tied
Your words lack proper pronunciation
The situation with your enunciation
Is you over-pronounce
Mispronounce
Words that they will discount
Because you're not confident in yourself
Why don't you keep your
words to yourself
No one else
Wants to hear your gibberish
And be subjected to malnourishment
'Cause your words aren't filling
Stop fooling yourself into thinking
you'll fulfill
The perfect will
He instilled
In you to use your voice
Why don't you make the smart choice
Be quiet
Be silent
Stop being defiant
Start being compliant
Mark my word

You'll never be heard"
Are you done or are you DONE
Listen Satan, this was "fun"
News flash, I've already WON
So you can get off your little soapbox
and go back to hell
Cause let me tell
You what you're not going to do
Continuously lie to me
Try to silence me
Rob me of my destiny
You have no authority or dominion
Your "power" is limited
In God I put my trust
You are crushed
Beneath my feet
Get behind thee, flee from me
In Jesus Name all will be well
So take your rhetoric back to hell
The fiery pit where you belong
Don't know why I listened to you
for this long
So long, get gone
I'm on assignment, on a mission
What God promised will come to fruition
Trust, everything I need,
God has already equipped me
So praise be to God,
I have the sweet victory!

A MESSAGE FOR YOU

God placed the vision in my heart years ago to write *Candid: A Memoir*, before it was even known by that name. Disobediently, I didn't heed God's vision until I received confirmation in February 2019. While attending a personal development workshop, I was challenged to use poetry to release the emotions I tried to suppress. My performance was subpar and paled in comparison to the other members in my group. I was playing it safe and not "stretching" like the exercise called for.

Ironically, I dabbled with poetry for years, but had never published or recited any of the poems I created. They were for ME; my raw emotions, my unfiltered thoughts, my bold self-expression, for MY eyes only. However, that changed because I changed. I realized that there was so much strength in being vulnerable. My power lied in my authenticity, allowing people to see ALL of me. Furthermore, my past didn't define me, it

143

refined me. It shaped and prepared me to carry out God's purpose for my life. He wanted me to use my story, my testimony to inspire others to live their truth and walk in their purpose.

Thank you for joining me on this journey. I hope it inspires you to unapologetically live your truth, free from shame. Give yourself permission to be your most vulnerable and authentic self. Boldly walk in your purpose and fervently pursue the vision God has given you. You are "perfectly" and purposefully purposed to do what God has called you to do. You CAN, I DID!

CANDID

A candid recollection and retelling of truths
buried so deep
Fighting ferociously to escape my memory

But God revealed and healed
What was concealed and tried to kill

ME
Relentless anxiety

Overthinking, fear, and depression
Caused me to hide behind a veil of
"perfection"

Masking my fear of rejection
Minimizing the valuable lesson
MY LIFE IS A BLESSING!

No longer ashamed
My testimony, my story, shall bring glory
To His mighty name

Not seeking fame
Simply want to inspire change

you CAN, i DID
Our lights can no longer be dimmed

Shine bright, live boldly
Purposefully & wholly

ABOUT THE AUTHOR

Sheryl Nicole Prince is an educator, entrepreneur, and author. Her passion for writing was discovered and developed in elementary school, around the age of 10. As an avid reader, Sheryl often found herself lost in books, a welcome escape from her harsh reality. Her deep love for reading sparked an interest in writing, and naturally helped her to hone her writing skills.

Writing became an outlet for Sheryl to express and free herself. Life experiences became journal entries and poems expressing her anger, hurt, pain, and inner most thoughts. In her darkest moments, writing illuminated her life. Now, writing to inspire change has become her gift to others.

Made in the USA
Columbia, SC
07 July 2020

12415557R00093